THE WONDERS AMONG YOU

31 DAY DEVOTIONAL

By
Brian and Amanda Trent

Table of Contents

ABOUT THE AUTHORS

Brian and Amanda Trent have been in ministry for over thirty years. Brian holds an MBA in Management and Strategy. Amanda holds a BA in Accounting and Economics. They have six children and four grandchildren. They are known on social media as the "Trent Tribe", a nickname they received years ago when all their children were small. Natives of Southwest Virginia, they relocated to the Lowcountry of South Carolina fourteen years ago to pastor Lighthouse Church.

INTRODUCTION

You may be close to giving up. You may have decided that you can't take one more day. You may think it's all pointless and nothing is making a difference. We just want to encourage you to stay another day. Deep in your heart, you know that you know that you are not supposed to quit, give up, or leave the place God has called you to. You may feel exhausted and completely depleted. You may feel inadequate and unqualified. You may feel like nothing is working out. We want to encourage you to push past the circumstances. We want to help you stir up your faith so that you do not quit too soon.

It doesn't matter how long you've been fighting, if it hasn't worked together for your good yet, then God's not done. Regardless of what the present situation looks like, you can sleep in peace, and you can have joy unspeakable. He is the sustaining one. He is the comforter, the healer, and the ever-present help in times of need. Do not mistake the battlefield for a graveyard. God has a purpose for your life and a purpose for where you are.

Stay another day.

Brian and Amanda Trent.

GOD SPEAKS YOUR LANGUAGE

Hebrews 4:14-16

Prayer is one of the greatest gifts that God has given us. Prayer has the power to bring us in line with God's will and direction and prayer has the power to bring God into a situation that is completely out of our control. Here's just a few things that I've learned about prayer that we should all keep in mind.

When you're praying, remember who you're praying to. There's this little boy at church one day and he went to the altar to pray. The old lady sitting on the front row overheard his prayer. She was probably just being nosy. She went to him after church and said, "I overheard you praying, and I noticed that you were not using proper grammar." After she spent a few minutes correcting his grammar, he said, "Ma'am, I wasn't praying to you. I was praying to God."

When we pray, we must remember a few things. Remember that God speaks our language. I'm not necessarily talking about English and Spanish and so on. I'm talking about you, who you are, where you're at in life. One of the most memorable prayer times I've ever had was done in a season that I was struggling with anger. I wouldn't have wanted anybody to witness what a hot mess my prayer time was during that season. Tempers were lost. Snot was slung. My grammar was not correct. But remember that God is not limited by your circumstances. God's not afraid of your issues. He will never look at you and say, "You have got to be kidding me. I had no idea."

Remember when you pray, you're praying to the one who breathed stars into existence yet was tender enough to make the rose bloom. You're praying to the one who owns the cattle on a thousand hills. He sees your need and he's more than capable of meeting it. But above all, you're praying to one who loves you like crazy and he proved that love through the cross. Hebrews 4:14-16 says, "Therefore, since we have a great high priest who has ascended into heaven, Jesus the Son of God, let us hold firmly to the faith we profess. For we do not have a high priest who is unable to empathize with our weaknesses, but we have one who has been tempted in every way, just as we are—yet he did not sin. Let us then approach God's throne of grace with confidence, so that we may receive mercy and find grace to help us in our time of need." God not only wants you to be bold in prayer, but he also cleared the path so you can be. Think about it, as a Christian, you have direct access to God, a direct line to the creator of the universe. Why not boldly approach his throne in prayer? Go be bold.

Love you guys,

Brian.

The Lord Who Makes a Way!

Isaiah 43:16-19

Where there is God's will there is a way. Just ask Moses. He stood in front of the Red Sea with Pharaoh's army closing in. He witnessed God making the impossible possible.

God's people did not arrive at the Red Sea by accident. God had been orchestrating this moment for years. Remember Joseph, the beloved son, sold into slavery by his jealous brothers? He went from slave to prisoner to prince. This dreamer's wisdom spared Egypt and his dysfunctional family from complete devastation during the years of famine.

Then there's Moses himself. He killed a man in defense of another. When it became known, no one came to his defense. No one stood with him publicly. Pharoah issued a death sentence for Moses. Moses fled to the land of Midian where he remained for 40 years when a burning bush moment directed him back to confront Pharoah. Year 41 came and at the age of 80, God called Moses to lead his people out of slavery and into the promised land. This trip out of Egypt only happened after ten horrifying plagues. Even after all that, Pharoah did not relent. The Israelites found themselves trapped between Pharoah's army and the Red Sea. One thing is for certain, Burning Bush moments where fiery desire launches us in pursuit of our calling will always be followed by Red Sea moments that leave us utterly dependent on God.

This Red Sea situation is no more an accident than the Red Sea situation that you're facing right now. The way ahead may seem daunting. You might feel broken and desperate. You can't go backward. You can't stay where you are. You also can't see your way forward. Trust God. "Thus says the Lord, which maketh a way in the sea, and a path in the mighty water… I will make a way in the wilderness and rivers in the desert." (Isaiah 43:16-19)

Whatever you are facing today, know that God is going to deliver you. He has a plan beyond your wildest imagination. Don't allow your Red Sea moment to become your Dead Sea moment. A Red Sea moment is not an end. It's a beginning. Life will happen on the other side of the Red Sea. We may have questions with no answers, but we also have his promises. Let your Red Sea become the proving grounds of your faith.

He goes before you. He goes behind you. He is in the middle with you. He fights for you. You can trust that he will bring you through. Where there is God's will, there is always a way. Trust him and move forward. Keep your focus on God – not your problems. No matter what your Red Sea is, God is bigger. Step by step, there will be a way. There will be healing. There will be restoration. May you have renewed faith to cross the Red Sea you are facing.

Sure do love you!

Amanda.

OVERCOMING STRESS & ANXIETY

Proverbs 12:25

Let's talk about stress and anxiety. I want to share a few things that I've come to realize and share something that will help you. It's something I've been doing for a long time. But when it comes to stress and anxiety, I've tried them, and they don't work. They're like pushing the gas pedal in a car when a car remains in park. It revs up the engine, makes a lot of noise, but it doesn't go anywhere. Stress and anxiety can't change our past and they can't control the future, although they can make for a miserable present. They exaggerate the problem, making mountains out of molehills. That is, they expand the problem, making it bigger than its reality. And finally, they strangle life right out of anything. The old English word for worry means strangle. But here's what I've done that's helped me. And it might surprise you.

Proverbs 12:25 says "An anxious heart weighs a man down, but a kind word cheers him up." Well, that's great news! I need someone to cheer me up. But it doesn't really say that the word must be received by someone else. What if that kind word come from you? So, when I start feeling anxious, I begin to make deposits of kindness in people's lives. I'll text something kind and encouraging to someone I know. Sometimes I'll go in their business just so I can share something with them. Just so you know, I don't say I'm here to share kindness with you because I'm feeling stressed and now, I feel better. They never even knew that I was stressed. But as I've done this over and over, I have found myself struggling with stress less and less. God's word is the truest form of truth that we will ever know, so reading it, living it and speaking it is life changing.

There's also an extra perk to speaking encouragement to others as well, one that we may easily overlook. When you're speaking kindness into people's lives, they don't dread seeing you come. They look forward to seeing you, which could also lower your stress levels. Think about it, when people look forward to seeing you, they will probably welcome you with a smile and embrace you with a hug or handshake. That could go a long way in helping to reduce stress and anxiety in our life. Imagine how much more amazing this world would be if we handled our stress by going out and giving away kindness.

Love you guys,

Brian.

HERE I AM

Exodus 3:4

A tiny seed contains within it almost all the necessary pieces to grow, to burst out of the ground into the beautiful plant it was made to be. But it will need nurture. It needs to be planted in good soil, to be given water, sunshine, shade. Then a seed needs time. We must wait and watch as what's always been becomes the fullness of what it was made to be. You are like the seed from which a plant grows: almost everything you need to be fully who you are is already inside you just waiting for those things that nurture you. Things that bring you life.

I don't know what season of life you are in today. Maybe you are graduating from high school. It's so exciting to celebrate that big milestone in your life that transitions you from childhood to adulthood. Maye you are a newlywed merging your life with that special someone. Perhaps you are a new parent with your new baby in your arms. Perhaps you are at midlife getting ready to make your next move. Maybe you are finding yourself in your latter years wondering how it's been so long since your own high school graduation. You are never too old to set another goal or dream a new dream. Wherever you are, whatever season of life you are in, you sit here containing within you all the necessary pieces to grow, to burst forth into the beautiful person you were made to be. And yes, at every stage of life from birth to graduation to retirement you will need nurture. To be put in places that make you come alive. To be given space to sort it all out. Tools to learn and grow and be. Learning is a lifelong adventure. Then we wait and watch as what you've always been becomes the fullness of who you were made to be.

God called out to Moses from the burning bush and Moses responded, "Here I am." Moses knew God spoke to him through the burning bush, but he doubted his ability to do what God asked. God called Moses to lead his people from a life of oppression. God had everything Moses would need to do what he asked. Moses wasn't eloquent. Moses had screwed up majorly. Moses was living a life of quiet away from all the drama. All of that to say, Moses is legendary. Despite all the things against him, he played a major role in God's plan to save his people. Oh, how we can relate to his apprehension. We all face times of fear or doubt. Even bible legends and heroes wonder, "Why me, Lord?" Yet our faithful God is there to remind us that He has been with us all along, and He will continue to guide and protect us. He works all things together to fulfill His purpose. We just have to say, "Here I am."

Sure do love you!

Amanda

SHAKE IT OFF

Genesis 50:19-20

Sometimes you just got to shake it off. There's an old story about a farmer and a goat. That farmer and his goat walked into town one day and he tied that goat up while he went in the store. Well, that goat ate through that rope and got loose. The farmer came out of the store and his goat was gone. He went and looked for him and he found him down this old abandoned well. He tried everything he could to get that goat out of that well, but nothing was working. Well, that farmer looked over and seen a shovel and he knew there was only one thing he could do. He just didn't want to see Billy suffer, so he started throwing dirt in the hole. And the more dirt he threw in that hole, the louder that goat got. After all that shoveling, the farmer turned around and there stood old Billy right behind him. See, every time that farmer was throwing dirt in that hole, Billy was shaking it off his back and stomping it under his feet. And he did it so much that eventually he had enough to get himself all the way out of the hole. Come on now, somebody needs to shake it off.

There's this Old Testament story about a man named Joseph. His brothers betrayed him. He was lied on, cheated, mistreated, falsely accused and thrown into prison. Kind of sounds like a country song, doesn't it? Every time something bad happened to Joseph, he would just shake it off and something good would come from it. By the time his story ends, he's gone from being betrayed by his own brothers and sold into slavery, to being a governor in Egypt. He had gone from the lowest of lows to becoming one of the most powerful men in Egypt and Egypt wasn't even his home.

In this life bad things are guaranteed to happen. But Joseph shows us that how we respond may very well make or break us. In this life, you will have dirt thrown on you at times. People will talk about you. Some will judge you unfairly. At times you may even experience betrayal. What will you do with all that dirt? That dirt can bury you or that dirt can build you. You're guaranteed to get dirt, but what you do with it is up to you. Shake that stuff off, stomp it under your feet and allow God to use it to make you better, stronger and wiser. Let God use what others meant to harm you for the good. Genesis 50:19-20 shows us the response from Joseph to his brothers that betrayed him when he said, "Don't be afraid. Am I in the place of God? You intended to harm me, but God intended it for good to accomplish what is now being done, the saving of many lives." Because Joseph remained faithful, God took him from the pit to the palace. Shake that dirt off and let God use it to take you places.

Love you guys,

Brian

WE KNOW HIM

Genesis 12:1-3

When God called Abraham, he called him to leave everything to go to a land he would give him. Abraham did not know where he was going. He had never seen this land. He did not know what he would experience, how he would get there, how long it would take, or what his life would be like when he arrived. Abraham didn't have to know the plan because he knew God.

Like Abraham, when God asks us to do hard things, we can because even when we do not know His plan, we know Him. We have been called by a God who has given us purpose, wants to equip us, and wants to partner with us to do something great while we're on this earth. We don't have to know how it's going to happen. We stay confident through God's word. We learn that he is faithful to do what he has promised. God's plan for us may be unclear but his promises are crystal clear.

We are a people who like to play it safe. We seek security in the plan. It's not our nature to act from faith. Safety and security don't come from come from God not our circumstances. Faith and peace occur when we cease trying to do things by our own efforts and simply trust God. Developing a strong faith that hears, believes, and obeys God promises isn't easy. It requires us to choose trust, practice patience, and surrender control. When we struggle to surrender control, we live in a constant battle with anxiety and insecurity. We can be overwhelmed by it. We might deny it, avoid it, and even numb it. We might think the way out of anxiety is to take more control, control of ourselves and others. We put more faith in what we can do than what God can do.

Abraham didn't have perfect faith. Scripture shows the things our spiritual heroes get right as well as the things they get wrong. Abraham made mistakes on his journey. The journey sure does have a way of exposing our shortcomings. Then we get the opportunity to work through them and overcome them. As we are able to surrender control and build our faith, we learn that God is bigger than anxiety and insecurity. God is the One who is ultimately supplying the power and resources. We don't have to take matters into our own hands. We just show up in obedience.

We may find ourselves saying, "I don't know how to do this. I don't have the money. I'm not good with people. I don't have enough faith." We can learn from Abraham's faith. God said go and Abraham went without hesitation. Abraham praised God beneath the stars even though he didn't understand how he'd ever become the father of nations. We can do the hard things because we know God. What is He calling you to move on?

Sure do love you!

Amanda.

TASTE FOR YOURSELF

Psalm 34:8

You ever had somebody tell you about a restaurant they tried and how you've got to go try it? There was a barbecue place in East Tennessee that was like that. People kept telling Amanda and I, that we had to go give this place a try. On and on different ones would go about how incredible the food was. So finally, one day we went and tried it ourselves and boy, were they right. You see, we tasted, and we saw for ourselves that it was good.

There's a scripture in Psalm 34 that says, "Taste and see that the Lord is good." Now there's a reason it says that, because we can't live off other people's experiences. I can't live off granny's faith, or mama or daddy or my neighbor's faith. I've got to taste and see for myself. I've got to have a relationship. There comes a point in time for me that going through the motions was just not good enough. I didn't come to church just so that I can jump through religious hoops so that I can leave as empty as when I came in. I want to know why people get excited when they sing about his goodness. I want to know why some people get excited when they read his word. I'm going to need some of that goodness. I want to know how some people can go through hell on this earth and still call God good.

See, because I've tasted for myself, I can endure. Because I've tasted, I can see, and the world can't take that away from me. Everything changes when you taste for yourself. We went back to that barbecue place dozens of times after that, in the rain, in the snow, in all kinds of weather, because we had tasted and seen that it was good. We have also invited hundreds of people to go with us, many of which chose to go. You see, we didn't do that based on someone else's experience. We did that based on our own experience. Taste and see that the Lord is good. It changes everything.

Love you guys,

Brian.

TIME TO SHIFT OUT OF THE DITCH

Colossians 2:6-7

I remember as a little girl being in traffic in an unexpected snowstorm. People all around us were sliding into the ditch. From little cars to big trucks everybody was struggling. My dad stopped to help, and I heard someone say, "Looks like everybody is in the ditch today." Someone respond back, "We all might slide into the ditch but some of us are about to shift into 4WD and get out of the ditch."

Have you ever had someone in your life that was dealing with problems, and you prayed for them, you advised them, you assisted them and then life took you away from each other for a while only to reconnect later and you find that person was still dealing with the same stuff? They had been stuck this whole time. Maybe you have even been that person before? Maybe you are stuck?

The truth is, we all end up in the ditch sometimes. We all face trials and obstacles in life. No one ever promised life would be easy, but God did promise to work it all together for our good. The problem is when we stay in the ditch spinning and spinning our wheels. We never shift into 4WD and get out of the ditch. We are just spinning aimlessly, without purpose, and without growing spiritually. When Jesus invites us to follow him, we don't know exactly where we are going, how long it will take, or what we'll encounter along the way, but we do know that he never leaves us. We were not meant to live life stuck in the ditch. We were meant to live life moving forward with Christ.

How we journey through unexpected circumstances depends on what we believe about the road we are on. We find hope when we fix our eyes on the truth about our journey and the one who sets our course. Don't spend precious time constantly complaining to others about how bad things are. That's time that could have been spent healing and increasing our faith. Time won't heal anything, if we aren't grounded in truth. We'll just feel worse as more time passes. Fixing our eyes on our eternal hope, keeping our roots deep in him, and building our lives on him will keep us strong in faith so we can shift into 4WD and get out of the ditch.

We can't control the past, the future, the actions of others, the opinion of others, what others think of us, illness, or how others take care of themselves. We can, however, always choose how we show up and how we respond. When we are following him, we are becoming like him. We become rooted in him, established in faith, and abounding in thanksgiving. Don't waste time wishing things were different or insisting that life isn't fair. Life was meant to be lived and life with Jesus is worth the living.

Sure do love you!

Amanda.

DON'T BE NORMAL

Philippians 3:13-14

Is normal what you really want in your life? Sometime back they paved the road coming into our town. Because they paved the road and they widened the shoulders out, they temporarily took the speed limit sign as you enter the town limits. It goes from 45 to 30 and many times you'll see an officer sitting nearby making sure we obey that sign. But I rolled into town like I normally do, and I slowed down like I normally do. It wasn't until well after I passed it that I realized there's not even a sign there right now. So technically one could get away with doing 45 into town now because there's no sign saying otherwise. But I got to thinking that I've done this so much that it's just normal for me to slow down. But this is where it gets interesting, because then I thought, could it be that I'm limiting myself and God because of past events, circumstances or things that people have said? They're like speed limit signs in my life. Let me give you a quick example.

I was 40 years old before I got my college degree because I grew up poor. I didn't think I could afford it. And because at best I was a C student, so I didn't think I was smart enough. And because nobody else in the family did it, I didn't either. So, I was allowing the past events, the past circumstances and the culture I grew up in to decide the present. From years of encouragement from my wife, I finally finished that degree. That felt so good that I went on and got a master's degree as well. But this is not about college degrees, it's much bigger than that. Don't put limits on your life. Don't let the past dictate the now. Don't slow down because it's the norm. Quit worrying about hurting people's feelings. If they can't be happy and excited for you for lifting the limits, then perhaps they're part of the problem.

Philippians 3:13-14 says, “Brothers and sisters, I do not consider myself yet to have taken hold of it. But one thing I do: Forgetting what is behind and straining toward what is ahead, I press on toward the goal to win the prize for which God has called me heavenward in Christ Jesus.” I’m not sure about you, but when I read that it reminds me that this life that we should be living isn’t normal. It’s a beautiful gift from God and it goes by way too quickly. Don’t let the past dictate the present or the future. Forget what is behind and move ahead toward the things God has for you. You’ll be glad you did.

Love you guys,

Brian.

WHEN PEOPLE THROW STONES

2 Samuel 16:5-14

Have you noticed that a child can be hurt by someone or something and they won't cry until they see mom? The child will run to mom's arms and it's there they cry. They eventually tell mom why they are so upset. My children do this. I've seen other children do this. There's safety in mom's arms. I think it is a beautiful picture of how God wants us to respond when we are hurt. Run to Jesus and pour out our heart to Him.

Many times, king David demonstrates this in the Psalms. He endured betrayal by friends, family, and people who didn't have a clue. When David was fleeing for his life because his son Absalom was leading a rebellion, a man named Shimei came out and cursed David and threw stones at him. When one of David's generals asked permission to take off his head, David responded by telling him to leave Shimei alone. He even trusted that by not retaliating against Shimei that God might return good to him in place of Shimei's curses. What an incredible response in such a difficult time! David protected himself from sinning by trusting God. David assumed that God's plan was beyond his own understanding. Shimei was throwing stones at David because he had bad information. He was making unfair and incorrect judgments. Ever had someone throw stones at you? Maybe a family member or a friend? Or even someone like Shimei that was misinformed? Words sting just as badly as stones, don't they?

When we look to the example of Jesus, we know those who crucified Jesus did it with the intention of getting rid of Him. But God used their evil actions as His path to provide for the salvation of the whole world. God can use the hurtful behavior of others to grow us, and it is God's responsibility to judge NOT OURS. We can remove that obligation from ourselves. Whew… That's a relief! After all, God makes for a great judge. He sees all and can judge rightly. He knows all. He can punish as needed. He is merciful and forgiving. We are shortsighted in our judgements. We don't see the whole picture. We can be quick to judge on bad information. We can be unmerciful when we are offended.

It's inevitable that challenging situations and people come our way. We will have stones thrown at us. The good news is that God's power and love is greater than them all. We can walk by faith and not by our feelings. What?!!! We CAN walk by faith and NOT by our feelings! Thank you, Jesus! Walking in our faith, we can be confident that God represents us and defends us. Um, does that sound as awesome to you as it does to me? It's totally God's will for us to live in victory. We don't have to live emotionally unstable and easily distraught.

Sure do love you!

Amanda.

WHO DOES GOD SAY YOU ARE?

Genesis 17:1-16

I read this over a hundred times, and I can't believe I missed it every single time. Could it be that we live up to the name that we are called? Because in the Old Testament book of Genesis, there was a man named Abram who was 99, hadn't had a child, and God had made him a promise. His promise was that he would make him a father of many and in doing so God changed his name from Abram, an exalted father, to Abraham, father of many. God also changed his wife's name from Sarai to Sarah. But you may say, how does this apply to me? I find this so encouraging and I hope you do as well.

Not only would God call them by their new name, but also Abraham and Sarah would have to call each other by their new name as well. And each time they heard their new name, they would be reminded of God's promise. Do you think they ever messed up and called each other by their old name? Sarah got mad and said, "Abram?" Abraham said, "Woman, that's not my name. It's Abraham. Get it right." You see, what God calls us is more important than what people call us. People may call you unfit, unworthy, a disgrace, or worse yet, by your past mistakes. But do you know what God calls you? God calls you his own, his chosen, his beloved, his child. I am a new creation. I'm blessed. I'm redeemed. I've been set free. This story from Genesis reminds me that we need people in our lives that will call us by what God calls us, not by our past mistakes.

When we respond to what God calls us, we not only walk toward those promises, but we also walk in those promises. There wasn't one single day that Abraham wasn't walking in that promise. It’s also vital to surround ourselves with people that will call us by our new name because as they call us by our new name, we are reminded of who God says we are. We are reminded of the great work God has done and is still yet to finish in our lives. One thing you’ll notice as you read this story in Genesis 17 is that God called them by their new names before the promise unfolded. Normally people call us a new name based on something we’ve already done or accomplished, but God was doing it in advance. God already knows the plans he has for us, so God and only God can call us by a name that corresponds to a promise that he already has for us. Just because I haven’t seen it yet, doesn't mean it’s not going to happen. Part of walking in that promise is knowing who God says we are and living each day by that new name. You are not your past. You are who God says you are. Don’t settle for anything less.

Love you guys

Brian.

PROTECTION IN THE WAITING

Genesis 6-8

We have all heard it, the story of Noah and the ark. A boat filled with animals and a rainbow shining in the background. It's a familiar story to anyone who has ever read a bible story book, attended Sunday School, or Vacation Bible School. In the story, we learn of a God-fearing Noah who was chosen to build an ark and because of his obedience to God his whole family escaped a devastating flood. Noah also became part of a story that even today teaches us about active faith, persisting patience, and full dependence on God.

Noah and his family built this gigantic boat according to God's design. It's interesting that the ark could not be guided or maneuvered in any direction by the passengers. The ark had no rudder. The ark had no sail. The ark had no compass. It's clear the ark was designed for survival. It wasn't built to go anywhere. It was built to just float along. Only God's mighty hand could guide the ark. It was meant to be a place of protection. Floating along was God's will for them at that time. Floating and waiting. How long? We know the answer because we know the story but Noah… Noah had no clue.

The ark story is our story too. There are times in our lives that we all need a safe place to wait out the storms that occur. Genesis 6-8 becomes a picture for God's people throughout history. In the storms, this is our reminder that God is our hope. It is this hope that gives us courage to persist. We are reminded that he is there with us. He will carry us through the storm. It is in the storm and in the waiting, we learn how to be a little more patient, how to close our lips, and open our ears. We learn how to let things go, to let things be.

We are not a people who like to wait. Many times, in our lives we don't understand why the ship is just floating along going nowhere. We might give God plenty of advice on what should be happening. We are probably even one of those obnoxious backseat ark drivers. Our prayers are likely even filled with navigation ideas that sound pretty good to us. We have a choice to make. Will we trust God? Or will we keep trying to steer this "massive ark" in our lives? Trying to be the captain of a rudderless ship is wearing us out and getting us nowhere. We must let God be God—for His wisdom and power are limitless.

Dear hearts, do not resent the ark. You are not forgotten. You can rest easy. You can choose to wait well. Your hope is not misplaced. Remind yourself of his promises. Remind yourself of his truths. God is faithful. God has purpose in the waiting. God is protecting you.

Sure do love you!

Amanda.

DON'T FAKE THE FRUIT

John 15:1-5

If you've ever found yourself struggling in your relationship with God, this might just help. So, when I first became a Christian, a lot of people in my circle began to say things like, "Well, now you need to quit hanging out with those people, and you need to quit watching those things on TV, and you need to quit listening to the music you're listening to, and you need to quit wearing those things." It was a whole lot of quitting. I heard it so much that I began to think that maybe I had messed up by choosing to give my life to Christ. Now, I'm not trying to be mean to the people in my life at the time, I think they were just telling me what they knew to be true. But I think they had it wrong because I did everything they said to do. I quit all the things that they said I should quit, and I still felt empty.

So, three years later, I pretty much had given up my relationship with God, and then I met this guy, and this guy was so strange, unlike any guy that I'd ever met before. And then I found out he was a pastor, but he was happy and joyful. At that time, I had never met a pastor that was happy. Now he taught me, and more importantly, he showed me that all those things that people had told me that I should stop doing and quit doing were fruits of a relationship with God. Not one single person had instructed me to build a relationship with God and to not worry about that other stuff. So, what I was doing was trying to appear fruitful by doing all the things that people were telling me to do. That's like planting an apple tree and then expecting to get apples off it the very next day. In other words, I'm faking the fruit.

Jesus says in John 15 verse 4 and 5: "Remain in me, as I also remain in you. No branch can bear fruit by itself; it must remain in the vine. Neither can you bear fruit unless you remain in me. I am the vine; you are the branches. If you remain in me and I in you, you will bear much fruit; apart from me you can do nothing." The greatest favor we can do ourselves is to connect to the vine, which means growing in our relationship with Jesus. As we grow in that relationship with Jesus, He will direct us in what needs to go and what needs to stay. In the process, we will be bearing fruit from a growing relationship with our savior. So can I encourage you today, instead of worrying about quitting everything, just work on your relationship with God and let God finish the work that He started in you.

Love you guys!

Brian.

ALL WILL BE WELL

1 Thessalonians 5:16-18

"All shall be well, and all manner of thing shall be well." Words by Julian of Norwich, whose book is thought to be the oldest surviving book written by a woman in English, written during a period of great suffering and uncertainty. The 100 Years War between England and France began before she was born and continued long after she died. Horrific famine was widespread throughout England. Rounding out the tragedy of war and starvation, as if those are not terrible enough, was a pandemic. In her lifetime, she saw the devastation of much of Europe's population by the bubonic plague. Three outbreaks occurred in her city. She herself nearly died from the plague. The heartache must have been overwhelming. Suffering was everywhere. Many attributed this horror to the wrath of God. Imagine the surprise, then, that her thoughts are not of despair or judgment, but of love and hope. She wrote of a remarkable yearning to fulfill the instructions given to us 1 Thessalonians 5. She chose to be joyful, pray without ceasing, and give thanks in all circumstances, however unpleasant and they were very unpleasant. She did this from her abiding faith that God works everything together for good.

Centuries later, we are still asking ourselves, "Will all really be well?" As our generation lives through our own pandemics, our own wars, and our own heartaches, I am both comforted and disturbed. I am grateful to have a happy home, a precious family, a stable income, a natural contentment to be at home, and a steady sense of hope. In my community, I see acts of bravery, generosity and love regularly. Despite these lovely life blessings, I feel grave concern, grief, and helplessness. They have become my daily much too heavy clothing. Living through current events that take our breath away, I find it hard to catch my own breath. No, in general, things do not feel well.

So, when Julian says, "all shall be well and all manner of things shall be well" it is not the Hallmark card statement of someone putting on rose-colored glasses or sticking their head in the sand pretending all this bad stuff will go away, but the voice of one who has experienced suffering and tried to make sense of it. The way she does so is through faith. "All will be well" is a statement of faith. I cannot pull out a signed contract from God guaranteeing that I and all those I love will be safe from major trauma or that I will triumphantly overcome all obstacles in my life. It is about something deeper and more inarticulate. It is an attitude that approaches this big, scary life with openness and hope rather than with fear and dread. It is a not a descriptive statement of now, but a hopeful statement of what shall be. A deep-rooted knowing that God keeps us. All will be well.

Sure do love you!

Amanda.

JOY MULTIPLIER

John 15:9-11

One day back a few years ago, Amanda shared a picture on her personal social media account that had four simple words on it that had a huge impact on my life. It said, “Be a joy multiplier”. Holy cow, I really like that.

Now as a believer in Christ, I think our joy tanks should be slap full and overflowing. Growing up, I would see these movies that had this portrayal of Jesus like he didn't have any fun at all and like his hair never moved and He always spoke in the King James language. But when we take a deeper look into the gospels, we see somebody different than what those movies portrayed. Even when he was born the angel said, “we bring good tidings of great joy.” In Luke 7, his enemies said he was being too joyful on occasion. That’s a problem we should all want to have right? They also accused him of being a glutton and a drunkard, even a friend of tax collectors and sinners. But in John 15, he says this, "These things I have spoken to you that my joy may be in you and your joy may be full." That's so good.

What if this world came to know us as joy multipliers? Let me give you an example. The other day we stopped in for an early lunch at our local Mexican restaurant and they didn't have our mariachi music playing. And we all know chips and salsa isn't the same without the music. So instead of complaining about it, I pulled out my iPhone and pulled up some mariachi music and started playing as loud as I could at our table. We were having a lot of fun and it changed the entire dynamics of everything. The next thing we knew, people were popping up from behind booths and employees were coming out and joining us.

You see, joy is contagious in any language. If your joy tank is full, and it should be, then you're going to splash some on people when you go places. The Joy of the Lord will overflow out of you and without even trying, it will spill over into other people's lives. People that have their own struggles. People that might be in a dark place and so desperately need to experience a touch from God. What an amazing opportunity we have, to be able to carry the JOY of the LORD with us wherever we go.

Love you guys,

Brian.

HEY YOU, DON'T GIVE UP

Psalms 18:32-36

We all love it when things are smooth sailing but in life there will always be rocks to climb, oceans to swim, and giants to face. The choice is yours: will you give up, or will you go through? Giving up means you won't know how close you came to victory. It could be that you are moments away from your breakthrough. Endurance is not about all the times you try and fail – it is the one time that you refuse to give up. It is not based on who comes in first but is reserved for the one who is determined to finish the race despite great adversity. You are more than a conqueror. Don't give up. Hang on. Hold tight.

Run to God's word and believe it's promises for you. We don't have to remind God of his promises. God is faithful. You must remind yourself of his promises. You must remind yourself that you can count on every word He says. "It is God who arms me with strength and keeps my way secure… You make your saving help my shield, and your right hand sustains me..." (Psalm 18:32–36).

Through all the hardships that you are experiencing, do not be shaken, stand firm and always remember that the place of your greatest resistance will be the place of your greatest victory. God always proves before He promotes. He is not looking for qualified people but rather those that He can work through. Remember that you are relying on his ability not your own. God did not call you to a task because it is something you can do. He called you because it is something HE can do. He did not commission His disciples because they could change the world. He called them because He wanted to change the world through them.

God is not limited in any way by your education, economic status, race, or social standing. God is not limited by your perceived inadequacies. Qualifications only matter to the world, not to the Lord. There is no such thing as the wrong side of the tracks with God. God uses ordinary people like you and me to do extraordinary things when we give Him our all and let Him do the work. The power of God is unlimited. God does hard things all the time, and he literally lives inside of us.

Are you on the verge of quitting? Be encouraged. Your struggle is literally on the verge of victory. Lean into God's promises. He will give you strength to endure this tough season. Whatever your battle, just don't quit. By faith, start seeing the victory God has in store for you. Believe what He says and keep Him first in your life. He will walk with you all the way to victory! If you look at the world, you'll be distressed. If you look within, you'll be depressed. If you look at God, you'll be at rest.

Sure do love you!

Amanda.

FAITH MAKES ROOM

Genesis 13:5-17

The problem is that I don't have room. Sometime back when our youngest son was seven-year-old he said, "Dad, could you hand this to me?" It was something important that he wanted. So, I went and got it and handed it to him, but he had too much junk in his hand to be able to receive it from me. I said, "Son, you're going to have to put something down if you want me to give this to you." Hold on a second. Could it be that the very thing that we've asked God for, you know, the very thing that we've been praying for, that God has it for us, but we're holding on to too many other things to be able to receive it? I mean, could it be that we're holding onto things that we shouldn't be holding onto and by doing so, we've not allowed ourselves to have room to receive God's provision or his blessing? Could it be that the good relationships that I've been praying for are right there, but I'm too busy hanging on to the toxic ones, so I can't receive the good ones? Could it be that I'm not where I want to be spiritually because I'm holding on to past hurts and not making room for growth in my life?

We have this saying at our house: "if you're praying for new shoes, make room in the closet." You see, faith isn't just believing that God can, it's about preparing ourselves for what God has. Ask Noah what faith is, and I wonder what he would say. Faith is first believing, but part of believing is preparation, preparing for what God has spoken, preparing for his promise. Noah could teach a class on that. Faith is also about God changing us in the process so that we don't carry around junk that we shouldn't be carrying around. Every time I take a step forward in faith, I'm leaving something else behind.

When you read the story of Abraham in Genesis 13, you see that his nephew Lot had been going wherever Abraham went. But there wasn't enough room for both at this point, so Abraham told Lot to choose a direction and go that way. As the scripture in Genesis 13:14-17 says, "The Lord said to Abram after Lot had parted from him, "Look around from where you are, to the north and south, to the east and west. All the land that you see I will give to you and your offspring forever. I will make your offspring like the dust of the earth, so that if anyone could count the dust, then your offspring could be counted. Go, walk through the length and breadth of the land, for I am giving it to you."

God didn't speak those words until Lot left, but as soon as Abraham made that space in his life, God spoke that promise to him. Wow! Sometimes we are all guilty of hanging onto things we shouldn't. Sometimes it's something from our past, like sin, hurt, pain or grief. But sometimes we can hang onto good things, like a good season in our life. We all love good things, sometimes so much that we will stay in a good season even though God is calling us into a new season. Good or bad, nothing is worth hanging onto when God is calling us to step out and follow him in faith. Faith will always make room for God's plan in our life.

Love you guys,

Brian.

CONNECTING THE DOTS

Esther 4:13-14

Remember connecting the dots as a child? The picture doesn't make sense by merely looking at the numbered dots. They are placed all over the page, zig zagging everywhere. The number one may be on the opposite side as number two, three, and four. Just like those pictures, you can never guess God's purpose merely by looking at the circumstances you are facing. The picture of the kingdom's purpose is only revealed by allowing him to connect the dots of our lives.

In the book of Esther, we see God connecting the dots of a girl's life in what look like a bunch of random events. As more and more of the dots become connected, we start to see a tragic story turn into a triumph. We first meet Esther as a young girl in a time when Queen Vashti gets cast away. Esther is selected to enter a beauty contest with all the lovely women of the kingdom. Scripture doesn't hide that these ladies are coerced. They are drafted. They aren't there because they decided to be. As "luck" would have it, the king chooses Esther to be queen. Then we read that Haman, the kings right hand man, is a racist. He hates Jews. He becomes enraged at Mordecai, the Jewish uncle who raised Esther. Haman decides to massacre all Jews. This Jewish orphan girl, now queen, suddenly has a profound and clear purpose. Mordecai meets with his niece to affirm, she really was born for such a time as this.

God's will weaves through time and circumstances like a pencil connecting the dots. Each movement may not appear to be leading to anything substantial until the entire picture has been completed. Every line drawn matters. This is why you must trust God even when you do not understand. He is always doing something bigger than what you can see.

Every step and every decision you make should be centered around the will of God. It's not about how much good you can get from God. It's to what extent you let him use you for the good of others. Where do you start? Every day all day long, you will see God's purpose unfold as you are blessing others. Start with your household. Your spouse, your children, and let it flow to your extended family, your church family, your coworkers, your friends, your community… This agenda is connected to everything he has given you to do. You are blessed to be a blessing. Like Esther. It's time you started walking in that.

Mordecai had to remind Ester of who she was, God is reminding you. It is God who has given you your job, position, resources, education… Don't miss your kingdom assignment. Boldly proclaim to our King, "Use me in whatever way you choose. Even in uncertainty, I'll take the risk. Just show me what you want me to do. Use me whatever way you choose."

Sure do love you!

Amanda.

INVITED TO LIFE

John 10:10

Here's where I screwed up. When I was younger, I thought that all I needed to do was invite Christ in my life and that would fix all my problems. But it didn't. But the preachers said that if I invited him in that everything would be okay. But it wasn't. As I've grown in my relationship with God, this is one of the realizations that I've had. When I say things like I'm going to invite him into my life, I'm making it about me, my schedule, my agenda, my problems, and the issues that I had, the anger, the resentment, the addictions, all that stuff just got worse. But isn't he supposed to fix all that?

But then one day I had a realization. I had been inviting him to join me in life, making it about me, and he had been inviting me to life. What? I began to realize that I had just invited him in to fix my problems, not to pursue him and that's a problem. Don't get me wrong, God wants to fix them, but I was doing it backwards. When I started pursuing the life he had invited me to, I began to pay less attention to my problems and more attention to the life that he led me into. And while I was out there pursuing the life he had led me into, he was back there fixing all my issues. Is that not crazy?

So instead of inviting him into our life and making it about us, we should pursue the life he's invited us to pursue. When we do that, God fills us up with love, kindness, gentleness, patience, self-control, also known as the fruits of the spirit. Without even knowing it, it forces all those other things out of us. When I stopped trying to force God into my agenda and started pursuing him and his agenda, he filled me up with fruit that pushed all that junk out of my life.

Jesus says in John 10:10 that "I have come that they may have life and have it to the full." Did you catch that? Many versions say, "may have life", some versions say "might have life". So, life is available, but only for those that decide to go get it. Perhaps it's time we stop asking God to bless our agenda and start asking God to lead us into his agenda, which we know is already blessed. Go pursue the life he has for you today!

Love you guys,

Brian.

THE DEEP WELLS

Isaiah 12:3

Water is essential to life. If we turn on our tap and there's no water, I can assure you, me and my house go into emergency mode. Shortly after we purchased our home several years ago, our water did stop running. We had to call a company that specializes in wells to figure out what was wrong with ours. Thankfully, it was just the pump and an easy replacement.

The average depth of a household well is 100-500 feet, but sometimes you may have to dig as deep as 1000 feet before you hit water. Today we have special tools and equipment that allow us to locate water, dig deep into the earth, and blast through rock. But can you imagine for a moment what was like for Abraham? When we read in the Old Testament about the wells that Abraham was digging, they were wells that gave beyond his lifetime. Generations benefited from those wells. He had to dig them deep and at times his enemies even covered them back up with dirt. His sons had to re-dig some of the wells he had already dug. The water from them was always good.

Isaiah paints a beautiful picture of a well from which the waters of life are drawn. It's deep in God's "wells of salvation" we experience the cool water of God's grace, strength, and joy. It refreshes us and strengthens our hearts. We can come to this well any time we want, and it floods us with joy. Today, as I spent time in prayer, the Lord reminded me to drink deeply from his living water, from the well of his salvation. I don't want to come to the well with just a cup. I want to come to the well with my entire vessel ready to be filled to overflowing. Life can be hard and frustrating. There are things that go wrong or cause us issues, but supernatural blessings and full life awaits us at the well.

I listened to a podcast recently with Dr. Edith Eva Eger, holocaust survivor, psychologist, and author. As I listened to this ninety-one-year-old share the extremely difficult circumstances she endured and share the loving ways she saw God even amidst the worst, I was reminded how important it is to draw from the deep well of salvation. It's what will sustain through hardships, pain, and grief.

You have an invitation to draw water from the wells of salvation every day, all day long. You can draw that water with joy! For all of eternity, you can drink in the satisfaction that's found in God. Maybe you are going through hard times. Maybe you feel empty or even spiritually dry. What will that living water do for you? What thirsts will it quench? What wounds will it heal? Don't just sip. Drink deeply. Live each day in the rich blessings of salvation. Praise God we do not have to remain thirsty!

Sure do love you!

Amanda.

DOES GOD GET TIRED OF YOU?

Matthew 7:7-12

Does God ever get tired of you? When I was younger, I worked at a grocery store. At one point, I had gone over 18 months without a raise. I was aggravated about it, and I would complain to all my coworkers about how I hadn't had a raise in a very long time. The regional supervisors were the ones that would give us a raise and they would come in the store about once a month. One day ours was in the store and I thought to myself that today is the day, this ends today. So, I went over to the supervisor, and I boldly said, "Mr. Supervisor, it's been over 18 months since I had a raise and I feel like that I am due a raise and he said, "Okay!" I said, "Okay? That's it?" He said "Yeah, that's it. You can have a raise." To which is responded, "Just like that?" He said, "Yeah, I was worried about you because you never asked for one."

I've complained, I've been mad, I've been frustrated all this time because I didn't ask. What a ding dong I had been. James 4:2 says, "You have not cause you ask not." It's the "don't be a ding dong" scripture. And you might've read Matthew 7:7 where it says, "Ask and you'll be given, seek and you shall find, knock and the door will be opened to you." But this is where it gets good, because that translation puts it like you just need to ask once, seek once, knock once. But that's not how the original Greek text puts it. The verb asks, seek and knock are all in the present tense. So, in other words, it's asking, seeking, knocking. That means I keep asking, I keep seeking, I keep knocking, because even in our asking, God does a work in us, not just for us. It's a work that usually leads to greater things than we are asking for.

So, does God get tired of you? Well, God just told you to keep asking, seeking and knocking. God can never get tired of you. So don't be a ding dong like I was when it comes to asking for a raise. Go ask. Go seek. Go knock. Keep asking. Keep seeking. Keep knocking. God will do a greater work in you than you could ever imagine that he would do.

Love you guys,

Brian.

TOUCHING THE UNTOUCHABLE

Matthew 8:1-3

One of my favorite things that I like about Jesus is that He touches the untouchable. Throughout the Gospels, he was breaking traditions because people are more important than traditions, and they still are. All through the Gospels, we see Jesus touching people and if we aren't careful, we'll overlook how powerful the simplicity of a touch is. In many cases, he was touching people that had spent years without the touch of a human being.

In Mark chapter one, Peter's mother-in-law was laying sick, and it says that Jesus come and took her by the hand. Mark chapter five, there was a girl that had no life in her and Jesus came and took her by the hand. In Mark eight, a blind man was brought to Jesus, and he took him by the hand. In Mark chapter nine, a father brought his son to Jesus and He took him by the hand.

We know that Jesus didn't have to touch to do miracles. Jesus touched because he wanted people to know that he was willing to get involved in their messy life because no one else around them was. He touched because he wanted people to know that he had compassion. So, if you ever find yourself or someone in your life asking, "God, are you willing to get involved in my messy life? Would you really want to help someone like me that's hurting, that's lost, that's addicted, that's divorced, that's alone, someone who really has nothing to offer?" The answer is YES, a thousand times YES and it will always be YES. He's a hand holder to those who have no one else to hold on to. He touches the untouchables because our mess doesn't scare him. When he holds our hand that may be in pain, he holds it in the pain, but his hand brings healing to the pain. While Jesus is willing to get in the middle of our mess, He doesn't walk away messy. Jesus is not changed to be more like us, we are changed to be more like Him.

Love you guys,

Brian.

RELEASING THE HEAVINESS

Matthew 14:26-29

Do you ever feel like you're carrying more than you can handle? Sometime back I saw this guy going through our town pulling a trailer behind his truck. What made this one unusual was the fact that he had a lot of stuff piled on that trailer. You could tell by looking at it that the trailer wasn't going to be able to carry that amount of weight. Later that day, I was going through town, and I see him again, but this time he was broke down beside the road. Just as I expected, the trailer couldn't handle the weight of the load and had broken down. He was traveling to heavy! Life can be the same way. Burdens, like our health, finances, family, our jobs, there's several things that can pile on us and weigh us down. If we carry unnecessary weight for a long period of time, well, we will break down.

Have you ever given a lot of thought about the story of Peter walking on water, especially when it concerns the weight that we carry? Matthew 14 tells the story of the disciples being on a boat that was being hit hard by the waves caused by the winds. In middle of that, Jesus comes walking along the water towards the boat. Verses 26-29 say, "When the disciples saw him walking on the lake, they were terrified. "It's a ghost," they said, and cried out in fear. But Jesus immediately said to them: "Take courage! It is I. Don't be afraid." "Lord, if it's you," Peter replied, "tell me to come to you on the water." "Come," he said. Then Peter got down out of the boat, walked on the water and came toward Jesus. But when he saw the wind, he was afraid and, beginning to sink, cried out, "Lord, save me!" Peter was doing just fine until he took his eyes off Jesus, but not only did he take his eyes off Jesus, but he began to turn his eyes toward the storm, the waves, the wind, and all the things that surrounded him. He began to sink in the water, almost like he had weight that he didn't need to be carrying.

When he stepped out of the boat, he was focused on Jesus. All those things that ended up grabbing his attention away from Jesus, all of those existed before he stepped out of the boat. The only thing that changed that caused him to sink was where his focus was. When his focus began to turn to the world around him, the weight of that world began to become so heavy that it almost drowned him in the water.

I want to challenge you today to read the story of Peter walking on water in Matthew 14 and as you do, pray that God will open your eyes and your heart to reveal the things that are weighing you down that you need to give to him. Maybe you can begin walking a little lighter today as you focus your attention on Jesus.

Love you guys,

Brian.

LET GOD DO HIS WORK

Matthew 6:33

If you're struggling in your relationship with God, this might just help. So, when I first became a Christian, a lot of people in my circle began to say things like, "Well, now you need to quit hanging out with those people, and you need to quit watching those things on TV, and you need to quit listening to music you're listening to, and you need to quit wearing those things." It was a whole lot of quitting. I heard it so much that I began to think that maybe I had messed up by doing this.

Now, I'm not trying to be mean to the people in my life at the time. I think they were just telling me what they knew to be true. But I think they had it wrong, because I did everything they said to do, I quit all the things that they said I should quit, and I still felt empty. So, three years later, I pretty much had given up on my relationship with God, and then I met this guy. This guy was so strange, so odd, unlike any guy that I'd ever met before. Then I found out he was a pastor, but he was happy and joyful. At the time, I had never met a pastor that was happy. He taught me, and more importantly, he showed me that all those things that people had told me to stop doing and quit doing were fruits of a relationship with God. Not one single person had told me, build a relationship with God and don't worry about that other stuff. So what I was doing was trying to appear fruitful by doing all the things that people were telling me to do. That's like planting an apple tree and then expecting to get apples off of it the very next day. In other words, I'm faking the fruit.

Matthew 6:33 says, "But seek first his kingdom and his righteousness, and all these things will be given to you as well." So I was being told to seek out being good. Basically I was given a to do list of things that would make me appear to be a better and more fruitful person. But what I needed to do was pursue the King, King Jesus. Seek him first and then these things would be given to me. Seek him first and as these things are given to me, the character flaws and issues and relationships would work out because God would do his work in me because of my pursuit of him. So can I encourage you today? Instead of worrying about quitting everything, just work on your relationship with God and let God finish the work that He started in you.

Love you guys,

Brian.

BLESS THIS PLACE

Jeremiah 29:4-11

Can God bless me while I'm living in a place that I don't want to be? Lots of people quote Jeremiah 29 11. You know the one that says, "I know the plans that I have for you, declares the Lord, plans to prosper you and not harm you." It's good, but there's more to it than that. This word come at a time when some of the Jews were taken captive into Babylon under the rule of King Nebuchadnezzar. So, wait, you're telling me that an encouraging word like that was given to a bunch of people that were exiles living in a land that wasn't even their own? That would be correct. You mean God give that word to people that were in a land that they didn't even want to live in? That is correct.

In Jeremiah 29, God reveals that he carried them to Babylon, not old king Nebuchadnezzar. The king really thought he was doing something, but it was really the hand of God. So, God told the captives that while they're living in a land that didn't want to be in, that they should build houses, get married, plant gardens, have babies, increase and so on, not necessarily in that order. But shouldn't we just wait on the Lord? After all, I'm living in a place that I don't want to be. How can God bless me here? But God goes further. He says to seek the peace and prosperity of the city. He also says for them to pray for it, because if it prospers, they will prosper. He didn't tell them to sit down and be miserable and curse the place. He basically told them to live life and prosper in a place that you don't want to be. Eventually, he took them back to their homeland and Babylon footed the bill. Nobody saw that coming.

You see, God can bless you right where you are if you choose to be a blessing and not a curse. Waiting on God is not simply doing nothing.

Waiting on God is being a blessing in the waiting. By being a blessing in a place that you don't want to be, the place you don't want to be may turn around and be a blessing to you. As you read the scripture from Jeremiah today, think about your life, your job, your circumstances. Have you ever complained about any of that? What if the blessing you desire to have in those areas of your life are dependent on you being a blessing? Go be a blessing where you are, even if where you are is not the place you had in mind.

Love you guys,

Brian.

HAS GOD FORGOTTEN ABOUT YOU?

John 3:16-17

Did you know that God sees you? Whenever I was young and growing up, I felt like that God sees me, but he's really just waiting on me to screw up and when I screw up, He's gonna pop me over the head with a stick or something. Obviously, I had a very messed up view of God, partly because of a few very legalistic people in my life that represented God in that way. But I later learned that's not the case, God wasn't waiting on me to screw up. I was relieved.

Back about fifteen years ago, Amanda and I were in this place in our life, spiritually and emotionally, where we almost felt invisible. Like maybe God didn't see us. Like maybe He had forgot about us and to add insult to injury, this happened. Our pastor at the time had invited this group of people from Michigan that would come in and just gather and pray for all the leaders in the church. And of course, all those leaders were invited to this meeting, except Amanda and me. We didn't find out until about two days later after it happened. Just to be honest, it hurt our feelings. But we're big people. We're mature, right? But here's what's so cool about this story.

Our pastor called me up and said, "I really have to speak with you today, if possible." That's when he told me about this meeting. But he went on to tell me that as they were closing this meeting, one of the ladies in the group from Michigan spoke up and said, "Do you have a guy named Brian that serves as a leader in this church?" Well, that got awkward. Once they collectively picked themselves up off the floor and confirmed that Amanda and I were volunteers in the church, she said "You need to write this down and give it to them." I still have a copy of that, and I'm going to spare you all the details, but I am going to tell you this one thing. Our pastor read it to me when I met with him in his office. The first thing he read was eight words that felt like medicine to my soul. Those words were: "God has not forgotten you. He sees you." Well, that went from hurt feelings to a lot of joy.

So, let's get this straight. God sent a woman from Michigan to Virginia to remind my wife and I that God sees us? We hadn't told a soul how we had been feeling. We put our smiles on each time we were at church and just carried on with life like we were perfectly fine. But God did see us. God sent a willing vessel that we still don't even know to this day, to deliver a word to our pastor so then he could deliver that word to us. A year later, we found ourselves pastoring a church in South Carolina, where we remain to this day. But now God has sent a couple from South Carolina to tell you these words: God has not forgotten you. He sees you. As you read and meditate on John 3:16-17, make it personal. God sent his son for you. That means that God pursued you and he still does to this very day. No one has ever loved you like God loves you. You are not forgotten, you are loved.

Love you guys,

Brian.

SHOULD I STAY OR SHOULD I GO?

Jeremiah 42:10

I just wanted to quit. You know, sometimes the hardest thing to do is just stay. I'm just keeping it real with you. We've been pastoring our church for over 14 years now, but we spent the first few years just wanting to quit. You ever just want to quit? Of course, I didn't tell anyone in the church at the time, but I have come clean about it since. We came to the church with a vision. We came into this with a plan and things didn't go anything like what we thought it would. Has that ever happened to you? Have you ever had a plan that didn't go the way you thought that it would? We were hurt. We were discouraged and somewhat depressed. It come to a point where I spent a lot of my day trying to figure a way out. I even bought a for sale sign for my house because I just knew for sure that God would not leave us somewhere that we were miserable…right?

But did you know that sometimes the most spiritual, the most holy thing that you can do is to stay? I mean, we talk about people doing amazing spiritual and holy things and we talk about things like walking on water, splitting seas, healing blind people, and shouting amen in church. But staying may be one of the most spiritually impacting decisions you ever make. Now, we're glad we stuck it out and stayed, but here's something that we learned: when things go bad long enough, it's hard to see the good in anything. It's like wearing glasses with stains all over them. Nothing looks right when you look out of those glasses. Even the prettiest things in your life look blemished and distorted. Then we entered in a new season where God cleaned our glasses off. He healed our hurt. He fixed my mistakes. He made all things new. In that season of staying, God changed us forever because we didn't see that God was shaping us during that season. Maybe that's where you're at right now.

Jeremiah 42:10 says, "'If you stay in this land, I will build you up and not tear you down; I will plant you and not uproot you…" By staying where God brought us all those years ago, we have figured out that God doesn't need favorable circumstances to do favorable things. God doesn't need big things to do big things. As tempting as it is at times, we cannot do God's job for him. Instead, God ask us to remain faithful and if we are faithful, he will reward us for our faithfulness. Where you are may not feel good, but it may very well be where God has brought you, not to destroy you, but because of what he has planned in that place. Don't quit on something that God has just started. Be faithful.

Love you guys,

Brian.

INSIGNIFICANTLY SIGNIFICANT

John 6:1-13

Have you ever felt like that what you do is insignificant and maybe even pointless? You aren't sure anybody notices you or anything you do anymore or counting that anyone even cares for you? Can I encourage you?

There's a story in John chapter six about Jesus feeding thousands of people. But there's an overlooked part that needs to be talked about. The story goes that a boy brought two fish, five loaves of bread for his own lunch. I like to think he was packing a Star Wars lunchbox, because a friend of mine in elementary school had one and he was the coolest guy at school. Andrew saw that lunch box the boy had and informed Jesus about the small lunch. Well, Jesus took it and fed thousands of people with it. Amazing right? But what about that boy's mama? What does his mama have to do with it? This isn't in the Bible; I just like to think about these things.

It is very likely she made that bread. It is very likely she packed that lunch. I wonder what she was like, and I wonder what kind of struggle she had? She gets up every day, she makes food, she cleans the house, she does all these things and then goes to bed and only to find herself doing them all over again the next day. Perhaps she whispers to herself at times, "I don't even know if any of it really matters because it's just insignificant." And perhaps while she was struggling with that, the very thing she had given away that morning was out feeding thousands. She just didn't know it yet. And what was it like when that boy came home and told her? What she had seen as insignificant became extremely significant from that day forward. It had been all along; she just didn't know it yet.

You may think that what you do or what you have is not much to offer? Your talent, your gift, it all seems insignificant. But here's the good news: Nothing is insignificant in the hands of God. Every single talent, every single skill, every single gift that you have was given to you by God himself, so let him have them. One more thing to notice is that when everyone finished getting all they wanted to eat, verse 13 informs us that they had twelve baskets of leftovers. What we view as insignificant in our life becomes abundantly significant when it's placed in the hands of Jesus. So go be significant today!

Love you guys,

Brian.

THE POWER OF GOD'S WORD

Hebrews 4:12

Let's talk about the Bible. A lot of people ask, how do I study it? Is there a devotional or Bible you recommend? Well, I've got some tips, but first let me be honest with you. I've not always been a fan of the Bible. It's not that I disagreed with it, I simply didn't understand it. The stories didn't make sense. The language was different. I'd put it down as quick as I picked it up. Then I come to know Christ at 17 years old and I still didn't read it. I'm just keeping it real. But then two years later, I met this guy who was also a pastor. And as I listened to him teach, I thought, wow, this is understandable. So, I read it more and more and I found that was sparking something in me. You see, the Bible isn't your normal book. It's alive and active, it's relevant in every season and every generation, it speaks to parts of our being that nothing else can.

More times than not, during a week, I'll get stuck on one verse. There have been times that I have read chapters in one sitting for the sake of accomplishing a goal to get through several chapters a day, but when I was finished, I couldn't tell you one word I read. For me I began to realize that it shouldn't be about quantity. It should be about quality and understanding. I think knowing the context of a verse is very important, but sometimes God will use one verse to absolutely transform our lives, at least he has mine. It really goes to show how powerful not just the word of God is, but how powerful one word from God is. There have been verses that I've read 100 times over the years only to go back and read it again to have it speak something brand new into my life. God not only spoke that word that we read, but God is still speaking through that word as we read it. That is powerful!

One of the best things I've done to kickstart my personal Bible study has been to pick up a good study Bible. I'm not endorsing a particular one, but a quick search online and you'll find all kinds. My first study Bible that I received when i was 19 years old was a "Spirit-Filled Life Bible". I have a few that I use today, but I still use that one as well. I must be careful because the original one is falling apart. But I love it because I have notes in it from years ago and I love seeing the things I was thinking in seasons from 30 years ago. What I have learned is that there are things that are deep within the pages of scripture that connect with things that are deep within us. Things that I don't think I would ever have been connected to if I hadn't have put that word in me.

There's also Bible apps that offer tons of versions and tons of languages that include devotionals on just about anything you could think of all for free. The Word of God is constantly speaking if we will take the time to just listen. It's not a tool to bash people. The Bible has so much life coming out of it, we can't even handle it all. Putting that word in our spirits will transform us, lead us, empower us and reveal the very heart of God. Just like we treat our bodies by feeding them several meals each day, we should also treat ourselves to the word of God numerous times a day. Building a thriving relationship with God will come down to how much we are allowing his word to speak into our lives. Hebrews 4:12 reminds us, "For the word of God is alive and active. Sharper than any double-edged sword, it penetrates even to dividing soul and spirit, joints and marrow; it judges the thoughts and attitudes of the heart." Plug into its power!

Love you guys,

Brian.

THE POWER OF GRATEFULNESS

Luke 17:11-19

In life we have a choice between being grateful or complaining. Does gratefulness have an advantage over complaining? Many years ago, I heard someone say, "gratitude is riches, complaint is poverty." Wow! That really makes you think about the things that come out of your mouth, doesn't it?

Luke 17 tells a story about Jesus walking along one day and these 10 guys called him out. Now these 10 guys had leprosy, a terrible disease that attacks the skin, the nerves, and can even disfigure the body. Traditionally, lepers would suffer banishment from family, neighbors, they were outcast. But these guys wanted Jesus to heal them. Put yourself in their shoes, wouldn't you also want to be healed and have your life restored? So, Jesus told them to go see the priest. Now that's kind of odd when you read it, unless you look in a little deeper. The priest was the one who would decide whether they were cleansed or not and whether they could enter back into society. Somewhere along the way, they were all healed. So, these men obviously had faith, and they were healed, but only one of them came back to express gratitude to Jesus. That one fell at the feet of Jesus and thanked him. And Jesus said, "where's the other nine?" But Jesus responded to that one and he said, "rise and go, your faith has made you well." He had already been healed from the physical, but it seems that he's being healed of something deeper. We must know that from leprosy, there had to have been a toll taken emotionally, mentally, and spiritually. I believe because of his gratefulness; Jesus went a step further than the physical and healed those things as well.

When we take the time to acknowledge the giver, not just the gifts, it's pleasing to God, and we get to enjoy a deeper healing. And all that comes from gratefulness. Something that 90% of the lepers left on the table. Question is, are we leaving it on the table? Remember that gratitude leads to riches that money can't buy.

Love you guys,

Brian.

THIS CHANGES EVERYTHING

Mark 5:25-34

Here's one thing I did to transform my personal Bible study time, and it may just help you. First, let me point out that the word of God is very powerful. It doesn't need my help to make it more powerful than it already is. I don't need to add to it or take away from it. It's alive and well.

One thing I did many years ago to ramp up my time spent in the Bible was to look for the stories, you know, the hidden stories, the ones that you can't really see. One good example is this story in Mark chapter 5 about a woman with an issue of blood. She had been sick for 12 years. She had spent everything that she had, and she had just gotten worse. Don't you think there might have been more to her story? I mean, perhaps she was married. Perhaps she had children. And because she was unclean, perhaps maybe they even had to separate because she was causing some problems for the family. I'm not saying that's what happened, I'm just saying she has a story. I mean, where was she living at? Was she homeless or what? I mean, she was unclean, so how long had it been since anybody even touched her or welcomed her with a smile, a good morning or I love you?

Well, why does that matter? Because this wasn't just a woman who was sick and had spent everything she had. I believe her whole life had fallen apart. She had missed out on things because of what was going on in her life, and she was desperate. And here comes Jesus. But see, because she was unclean, she couldn't go to the temple. And this woman broke the rules and pressed in. Haven't you ever been so desperate you're willing to break the rules? Which reveals something else in the story. You see, up until now God's dwelling place was in the temple. But Jesus is proof that God is now dwelling among people. Well, this changes everything. Because of this woman's desperation, her brokenhearted story reveals to me and you that we have the same access that she had. We don’t have to go through a man or a building to get that access, because that access to God comes through Jesus. Jesus is proof that God will meet me right where I'm at and just like her, our life will never be the same. I hope that encourages you today. Whether you find yourself desperate or not, I pray that you will press into him like she did. Press through the noise in your life, press through the crowded spaces in your life, press through and get to Jesus. If we find Jesus, we find the Father.

Love you guys,

Brian.

Made in the USA
Monee, IL
12 November 2024